THE KILLERS DAY & AGE

Music arranged by Derek Jones.
Music processed by Paul Ewers Music Design.
Edited by Fiona Bolton.

Artwork/paintings by Paul Normansell.
Original package design by Julian Peploe Studio.

ISBN: 978-1-4234-8198-0

HAL•LEONARD® CORPORATION

7777 W. BLUEMOUND RD. P.O. BOX 13819 MILWAUKEE, WI 53213

Printed in the EU.

For all works contained herein:
Unauthorized copying, arranging, adapting, recording, Internet posting,
public performance, or other distribution of the printed music in this
publication is an infringement of copyright.
Infringers are liable under the law.

Visit Hal Leonard Online at
www.halleonard.com

LOSING TOUCH

Lyrics by Brandon Flowers
Music by Brandon Flowers, Dave Keuning,
Mark Stoermer & Ronnie Vannucci

Original key G♯ minor

♩ = 116

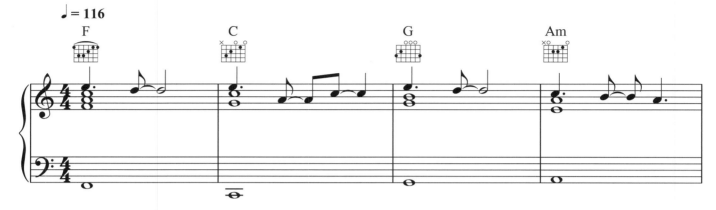

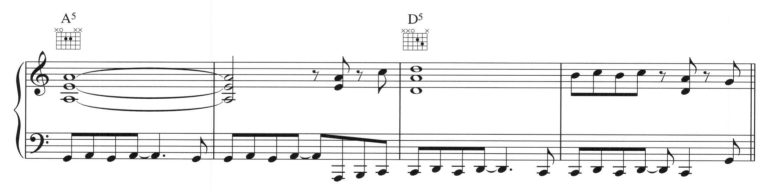

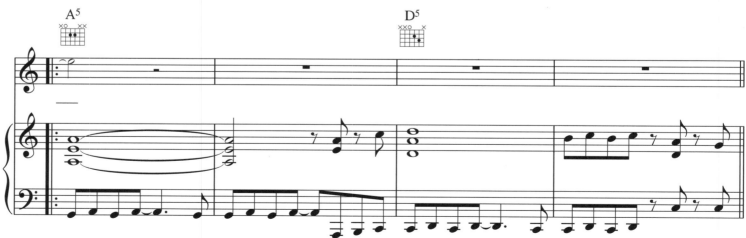

© Copyright 2008 Universal Music Publishing Limited.
All rights in Germany administered by Universal Music Publ. GmbH.
All Rights Reserved. International Copyright Secured.

I heard you found a wish-ing well__ in the ci - ty.

Con-sole me in my dark-est hour.__ Then you throw me down.__

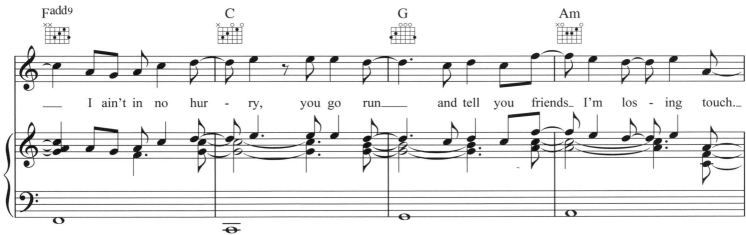

__ I ain't in no hur-ry, you go run__ and tell you friends__ I'm los-ing touch.__

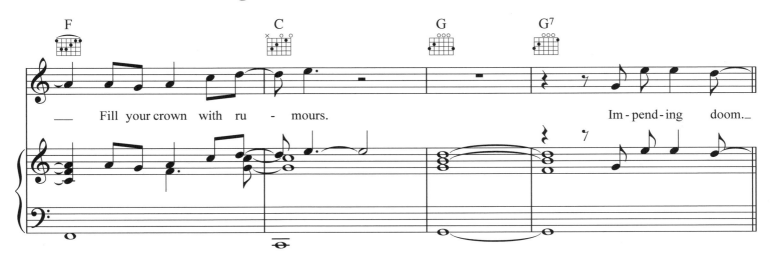

__ Fill your crown with ru - mours. Im-pend-ing doom.__

HUMAN

Lyrics by Brandon Flowers

Music by Brandon Flowers, Dave Keuning,
Mark Stoermer & Ronnie Vannucci

© Copyright 2008 Universal Music Publishing Limited.
All rights in Germany administered by Universal Music Publ. GmbH.
All Rights Reserved. International Copyright Secured.

-man   or are we dan-cer?   My sign is vi-

-tal,   my hands are cold.___   And I'm on my knees___

___ look-ing for the an - swer.___   Are we

hu - man___   or are we dan - cer?___

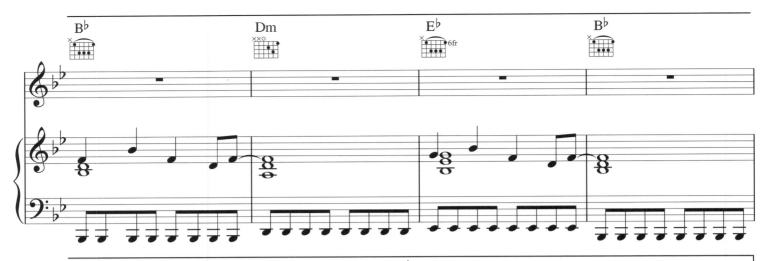

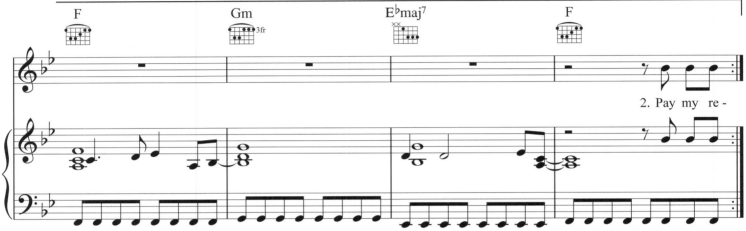

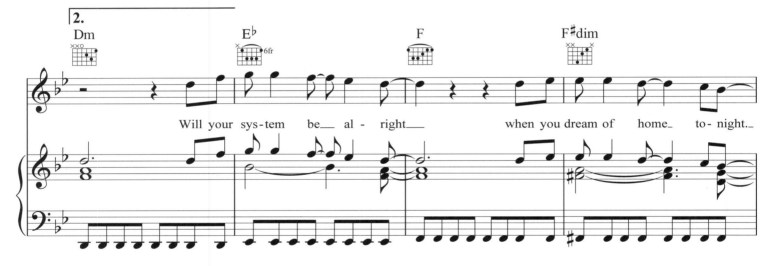

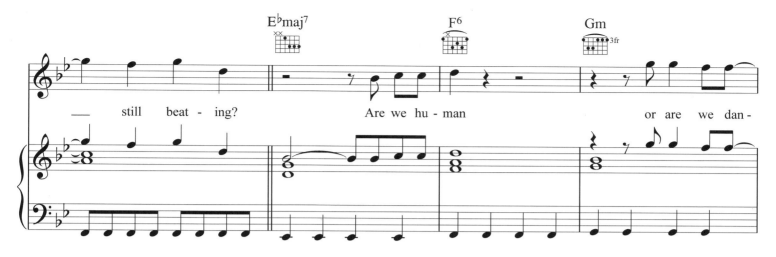

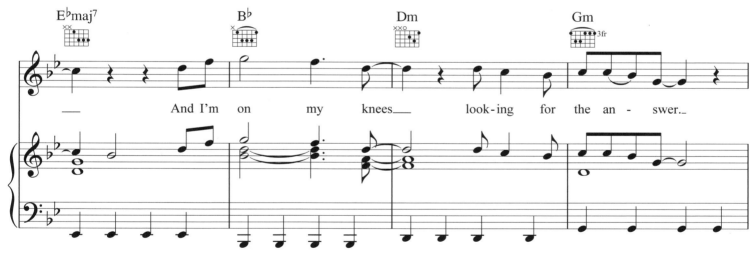

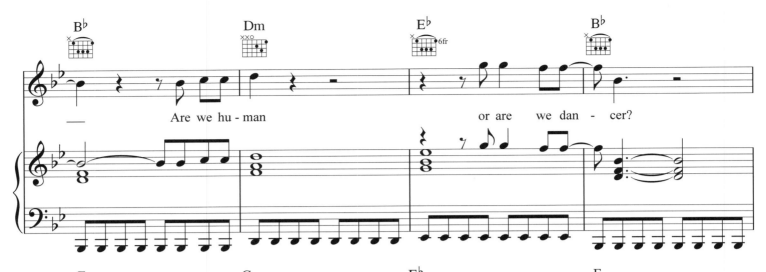

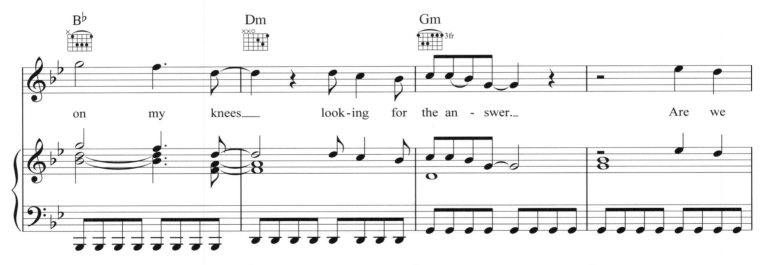

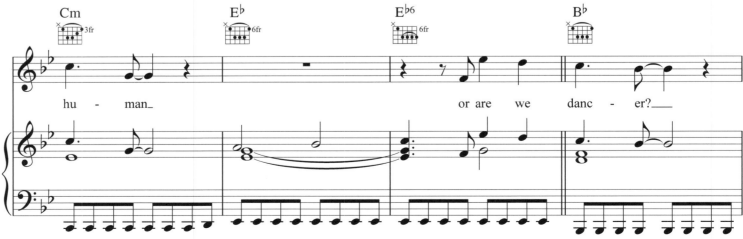

Instrumental ad lib.

Are we hu - man_ or are we dan - cer?_ Are we

hu - man_ or are we dan - cer?_

Repeat and fade

SPACEMAN

Lyrics by Brandon Flowers

Music by Brandon Flowers, Dave Keuning,
Mark Stoermer & Ronnie Vannucci

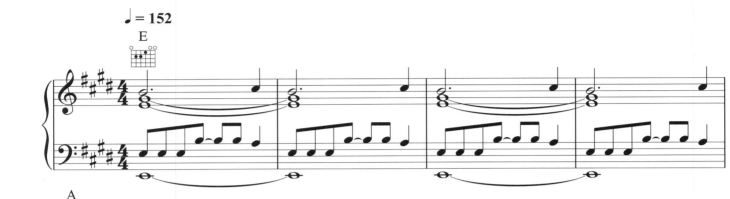

Oh oh oh— oh— oh oh.— Oh oh oh— oh— oh oh.—

Oh oh oh— oh— oh oh.— Oh oh oh— oh— oh oh.—

© Copyright 2008 Universal Music Publishing Limited.
All rights in Germany administered by Universal Music Publ. GmbH.
All Rights Reserved. International Copyright Secured.

N.C.

1. It start-ed with a low - light. Next thing I knew they ripped_
2. Well, now I'm back at home_ and I'm look-ing for-ward to_

_ me from my bed_ and then they took my blood - type.
_ this life_ I live._ You know it's gon-na harm_ me,

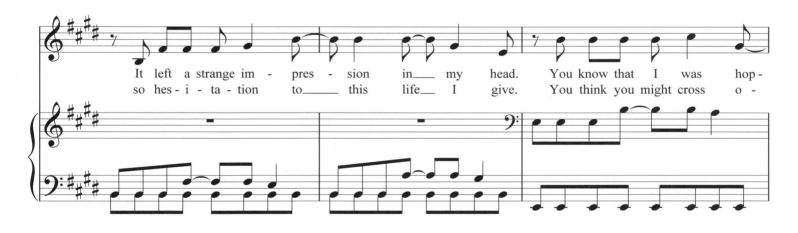

It left a strange im - pres - sion in_ my head. You know that I was hop-
so hes - i - ta - tion to_ this life_ I give. You think you might cross o -

-ing, that I could leave this star - crossed world_ be - hind,_
-ver, you're caught be - tween the dev - il and the deep blue sea._

21

____ but when they cut me o - pen
____ You'd bet - ter look it o - ver.

I guess I changed my mind.___
Be-fore you make that leap.___

A

B

____ And you know I____ might____ have just
____ And you know I'm____ fine,____ but I

C#m　**G#m**　**A**　**B**

flown too____ far____ from the floor this____ time.　'Cause they're
hear those____ voic - es at night. Some - times they

C#m　**G#**　**A**

call - ing me by____ my name.____　And they're zip - ping white light beams,
jus - ti - fy____ my claim.____　And the pub - lic don't dwell on

The star-mak-er says it ain't so bad. The dream-mak-er's gon-na make you mad.

The space-man says ev-'ry-bod-y look down. It's all in your mind.

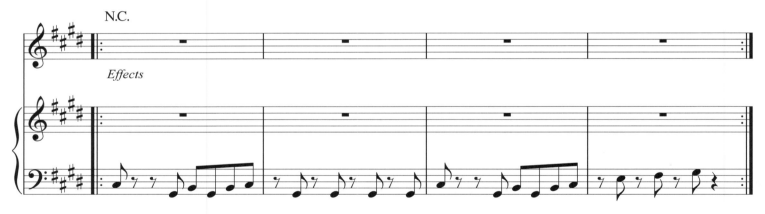

Effects

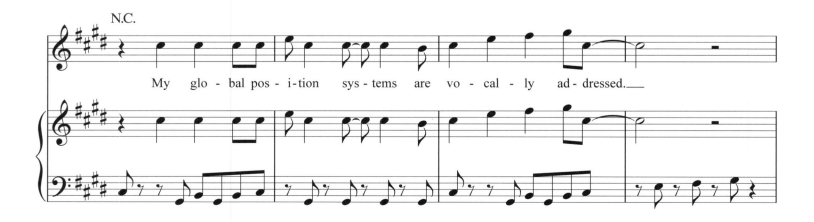

My glo-bal pos-i-tion sys-tems are vo-cal-ly ad-dressed.

They say the Nile_ used_ to run__ from east to west.__

They say the Nile_ used_ to run__ from east to west._

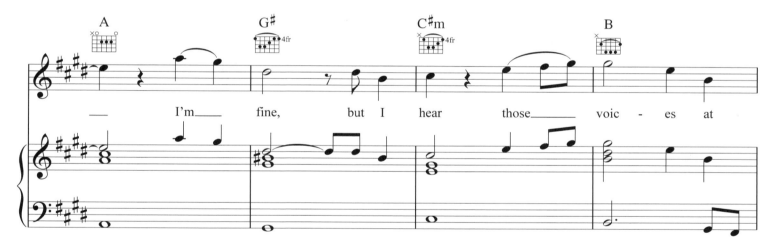

__ I'm__ fine, but I hear those__ voic - es at

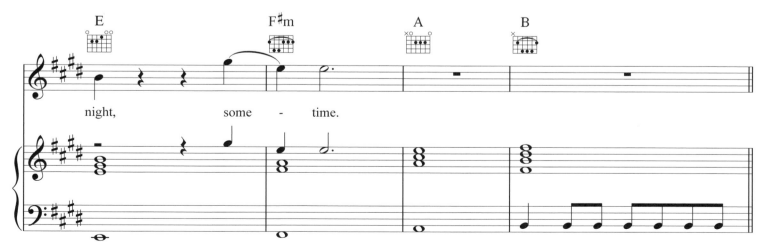

night, some - time.

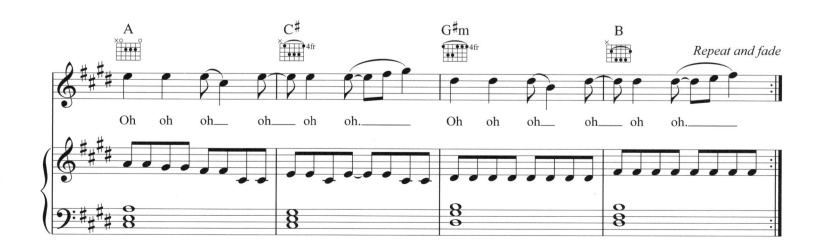

JOY RIDE

Lyrics by Brandon Flowers

Music by Brandon Flowers, Dave Keuning,
Mark Stoermer & Ronnie Vannucci

© Copyright 2008 Universal Music Publishing Limited.
All rights in Germany administered by Universal Music Publ. GmbH.
All Rights Reserved. International Copyright Secured.

win.____ (Joy____ ride.) There's

some-thing in the dis - tance, a glo - ri - ous ex - ist - ence

A sim - ple cel - e - bra - tion, a

place you nev - er been_ be - fore.____ Tell me that you want_ it

low, joy ride. (Joy ride.)

All your hopes and dreams,___

all you need to know.___ Joy___ ride.___

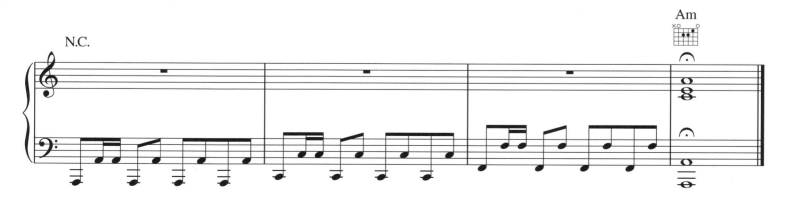

A DUSTLAND FAIRYTALE

Lyrics by Brandon Flowers
Music by Brandon Flowers, Dave Keuning,
Mark Stoermer & Ronnie Vannucci

© Copyright 2008 Universal Music Publishing Limited.
All rights in Germany administered by Universal Music Publ. GmbH.
All Rights Reserved. International Copyright Secured.

blue jean___ ser - e - nade.___ Moon Riv - er what'd you do to me?___

I don't be - lieve you.___ Saw Cin - der - el - la in a par - ty dress,___

___ but she was look - ing for a night - gown.___ I saw the dev - il wrap - ping up his hands.___

___ He's get - ting read - y for the show - down.___ I saw the min - ute that I turned a - way___

35

I got my mon-ey on a palm to-night._____ A

♩ = 136

change came in dis - guise_____ of rev - e - la - tion, set_____ his soul_____

_____ on fire._____ She says she al - ways knew_____ he'd come a - round._____

And the dec - ades dis - ap - pear_____

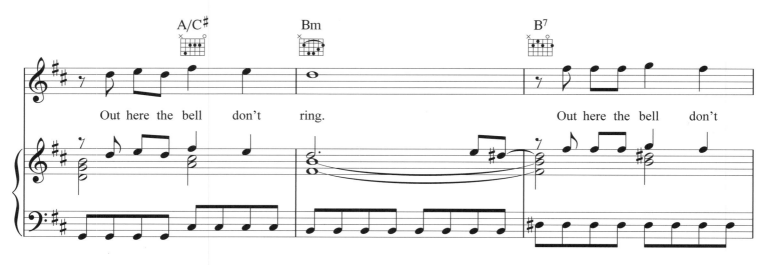

Out here the bell don't ring. Out here the bell don't

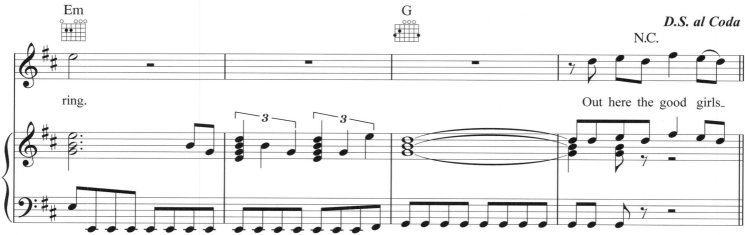

D.S. al Coda

ring. Out here the good girls

Coda

Out where the dreams are high.

THIS IS YOUR LIFE

Lyrics by Brandon Flowers

Music by Brandon Flowers, Dave Keuning,
Mark Stoermer & Ronnie Vannucci

© Copyright 2008 Universal Music Publishing Limited.
All rights in Germany administered by Universal Music Publ. GmbH.
All Rights Reserved. International Copyright Secured.

Can - dy talks_ to stran - gers. Thinks her life's_ in dan - ger.

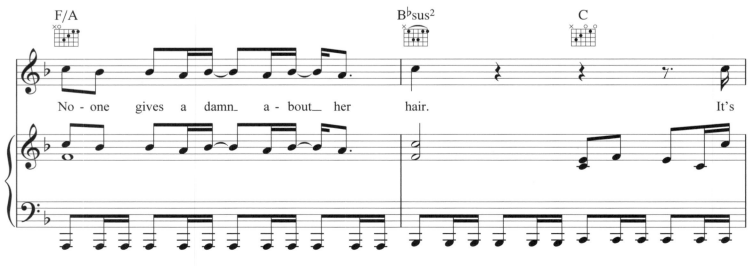

No - one gives a damn_ a - bout_ her hair. It's

Wait for some - thing bet - ter. No - one be - hind____

____ you watch - ing your shad - ows. This feel - ing won't

go.

I CAN'T STAY

Lyrics by Brandon Flowers
Music by Brandon Flowers, Dave Keuning,
Mark Stoermer & Ronnie Vannucci

© Copyright 2008 Universal Music Publishing Limited.
All rights in Germany administered by Universal Music Publ. GmbH.
All Rights Reserved. International Copyright Secured.

No, I nev-er made the time. In the dark

for a while now. I can't stay so

far. I can't stay much long - er.

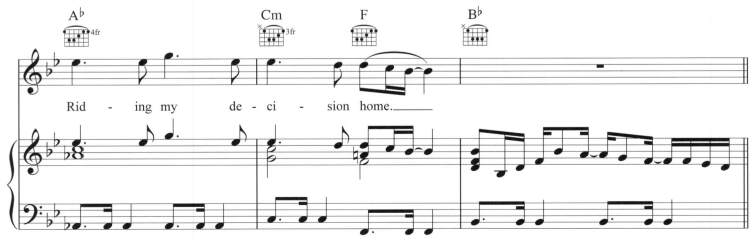

Rid - ing my de - ci - sion home.

Ex-on-er-a-tion lost_ its e - ra - ser, but my for-giv-er found a

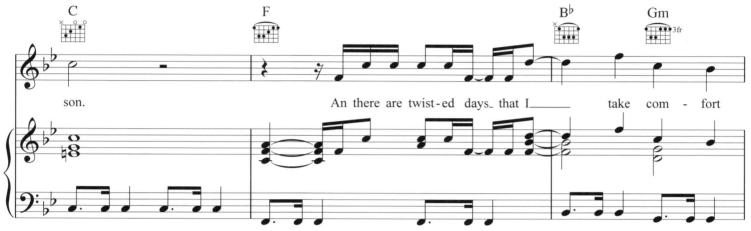

son. An there are twist-ed days_ that I_____ take com - fort

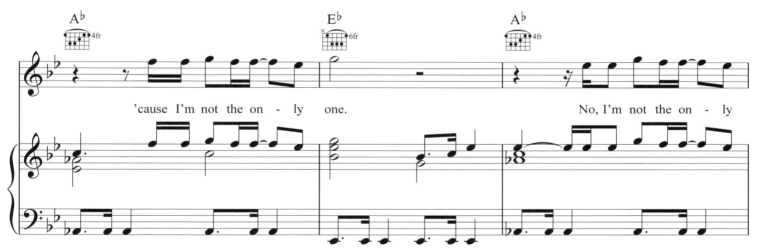

'cause I'm not the on - ly one. No, I'm not the on - ly

one. In the dark____ for a while_

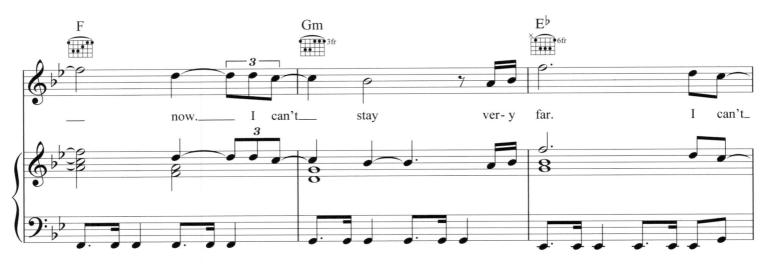

now.___ I can't___ stay ver-y far. I can't__

___ stay much long - er. Rid - ing my de-

-ci - sion home.___

Now there's a maj-es-ty___ at my door-step. And there's a lit-tle boy__ in

her arms._____ I will pa-rade a-round with - out game-plans,

ob-li-ga-tion or a-larm._____ In the dark__

__ for a while now. I can't__ stay__ ver-y far. I can't__

Repeat and fade

__ stay__ much long - er. Rid - ing my de - ci - sion home. In the dark__

NEON TIGER

Lyrics by Brandon Flowers
Music by Brandon Flowers, Dave Keuning,
Mark Stoermer & Ronnie Vannucci

© Copyright 2008 Universal Music Publishing Limited.
All rights in Germany administered by Universal Music Publ. GmbH.
All Rights Reserved. International Copyright Secured.

B

We bring you the wild - er side__ of gold and glitz.__

% **F#**   **G#m**   **E**   **F#/A#**

Run, ne - on ti - ger, there's a lot on your__ mind.__
Run, ne - on ti - ger, there's a lot on your__ mind.__
% Run, ne - on ti - ger, there's a price on your__ head.__

F#   **B**   **G#**

They pro-mised just to pet__ you,____ but don't you let 'em get__ you.____ A -
They stra - te - gise and name__ you,____ but don't you let 'em tame__ you.____ You're
They'll hunt you down and gut__ you,____ I'll nev - er let 'em touch__ you.____ A -

E   **D#m**   **F#**   *To Coda* ⊕

- way, a - way oh, one. Un - der the heat__
far too pure and bold to suf - fer the strain__
- way, a - way, oh, one. I'm beg-ging you ne -

55

Give me roll-ing hills_ and to-night could be the night that I stand a-mong the thou-sand thrills.

Mis-ter, cut me some slack_'cause I don't wan-na go back. I want a new day and age._

Come on girls_ and boys,_ ev-'ry-one make some noise._

D.S. al Coda

THE WORLD WE LIVE IN

Lyrics by Brandon Flowers
Music by Brandon Flowers, Dave Keuning,
Mark Stoermer & Ronnie Vannucci

© Copyright 2008 Universal Music Publishing Limited.
All rights in Germany administered by Universal Music Publ. GmbH.
All Rights Reserved. International Copyright Secured.

got-ta be-lieve___ it's worth___ it, with-out a vic-to-ry___ I'm so

sanc-ti-fied and free.___ Well, may-be I'm just___ mis-tak-

-en.

cont. sim.

The les-son learned and the wheels keep turn-ing.

GOODNIGHT, TRAVEL WELL

Lyrics by Brandon Flowers
Music by Brandon Flowers, Dave Keuning,
Mark Stoermer & Ronnie Vannucci

© Copyright 2008 Universal Music Publishing Limited.
All rights in Germany administered by Universal Music Publ. GmbH.
All Rights Reserved. International Copyright Secured.

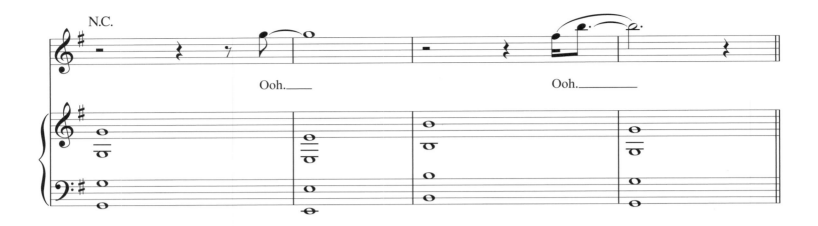

Ooh._____ Ooh._____

And all that stands be-tween_ the soul's_ re-lease,_ this tem-po-ra - ry flesh and bone._

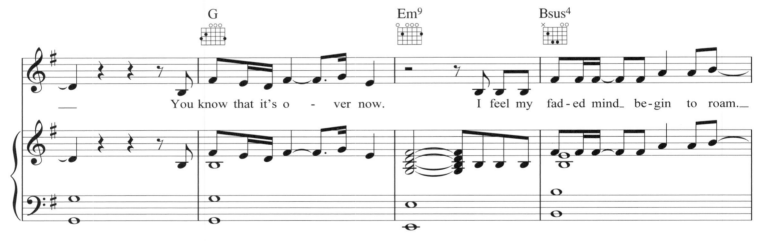

G   Em⁹   Bsus⁴

_ You know that it's o - ver now. I feel my fad-ed mind_ be-gin to roam._

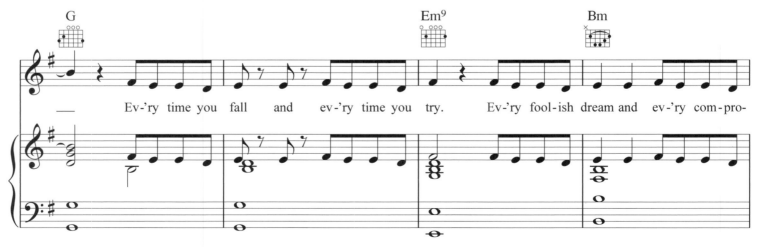

G   Em⁹   Bm

_ Ev-'ry time you fall and ev-'ry time you try. Ev-'ry fool-ish dream and ev-'ry com-pro-

G   Em⁹

- mise.   Ev - 'ry word you've spo - ken, ev - 'ry - thing you said.   Ev - 'ry - thing you

Bm   G   G

left me, ram - bles in my head.___   And there's noth - ing I can say.

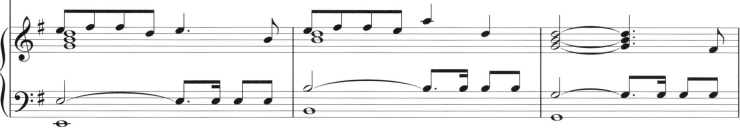

Em⁹   Bm   G

There's noth - ing I can do now.   There's

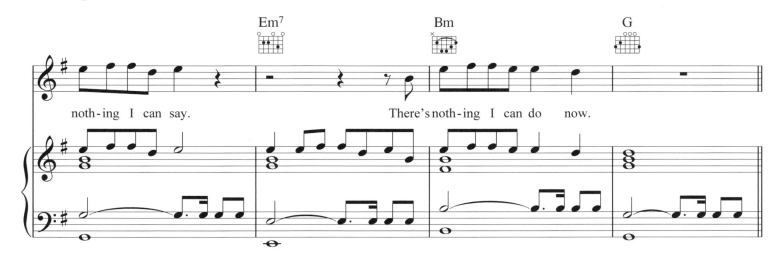

             Em⁷   Bm   G

noth - ing I can say.   There's noth - ing I can do now.

noth-ing I can say._____ There's noth-ing I can do now._____ There's

noth-ing I can say._____ There's noth-ing we can do now. Good -

- night._____ Tra - - vel well.____ Good -

- night._____ Tra - - vel well.___ And there's

1 2 3 4 5 6 7 8 9

AM997865